FIRSTMATTERPRESS
Portland, Ore.

SUSPENDED
IN MY
INSECTICIDE
JAR

SUSPENDED IN MY INSECTICIDE JAR

clara mcauley

FIRSTMATTERPRESS
Portland, Ore.

First Edition

Published in the United States
by First Matter Press
Portland, Oregon

Paperback ISBN-13: 978-1-958600-08-5
Library of Congress Control Number: 2024940358

This project was funded in part by Literary Arts'
Oregon Literary Fellowship for Publishers.
literary-arts.org

Editors: Hailey Spencer & Emily Moon
Contributing Editors: ash good & Lauren Paredes
In Cohort: Sophie Hall
Contributing Readers: Sky Mykland & Andra Vltavín
Copy Editor: Andra Vltavín

Cover: *Jar of Moths*
36 inches x 48 inches (charcoal and oil on canvas)
Copyright © 2024 by Alexandra Strenfel
alexandrastrenfel.com

Book design by ash good
ashgood.com

For all the people and poets who feel like an eclipse of moths.
You deserve to be here. You are seen.

POEMS

Only dead people write memoirs,

drag themselves into an epilogue as if there is nothing left to talk about. Poets, on the other hand, find beginnings amid everything. We are titled with tooth, hair, and nail, the kinds of keratin crime scene traces that aren't quite painless. After that, we bury the rest of ourselves beneath pages, leave caesura in skin and plant drops of ink in the incisions, flow like unfinished prose, write until we have been spilled and jarred and salt-dried and revived, until we have briefly drowned out that winged, irregular beat, that tiny corner of the heart that will always want to die;

persona

pretty girl, stop talking to your skeleton, your warped reflection.
leave your face in its puddle on the floor and let the ripples paint it
over, stranded like a ghost moth in an ether-laced jar, like a dead fish
with pale eyes rolled back in its head, with scales that embed themselves
in the mesh of cast nets. speaking of eyes, pretty girl, I have seen that
look before; I know how your pupils burned and how they were doused,
how the cold night sky swallows pearls and spits out pebbles. I know
that the dark made it hard to rearrange yourself, had you on your knees
fumbling for vertebrae and fallen knuckles; you keep going to pieces,
pretty girl, and you were never one for puzzles. still, you seem to have
mastered your craft, your masquerade beneath alloys of resin and
porcelain and ribbons wrapped around your neck like satin gills; do
they hold your head on, pretty girl, or are they just a bandage for your
jigsaw skin? oh yes, it is not hard to recognize an edifice of artifice, a
scalpful of strings, every taxidermy specimen has its mouthful of winged
insects, and you speak them, pretty girl, I see how you scream, I see
the crack that runs across your forehead. does that stone expression
ever grow heavy? for just a second, drop your smile and show me what
is underneath.

Honeycomb Girl

Cut crosswise: find hive insides, honeycomb girl pockmarked by the hexagonal collapse of her own architecture.

It began with jarfuls: absences and small gaps where walls intersect, sold at farmers market price until she grew used to the emptiness, mastered the precise balance of burrowing fingers into waxen scaffolding and harvesting the dripping citrine, tapped the inner workings of a shelved commodity.

What is left: sticky cuticles and a kaleidoscope of cut glass, plundered sanctum stamped by pressed faces and adjacent puncture wounds, hornet moth corpses in crumpled tissue, insecticide-spiked.

What is: a trypophobic's edifice, torn open by organized swarms of tourism, again and again, the decimation of saccharine framework, remains contained by the stretching of surface tension across hollow chambers and horizontal wells of amber.

She is: a most precarious structure, the girl who kept on gambling against catalysts, the girl who became an apiary of abrasions.

Bellies

Body always sounded like a bad word
to me
too round in my mouth
as if it would fall out
like a button from a conspicuously split seam.
And so what? If I didn't think I had to live
with this soft belly and bloody lip
so what if I went hungry
so what
if I wanted
to feel beautiful
once
to glance into that secondhand mirror
that I cracked, not nearly seven years ago
and see a glowing girl reflected back
instead of a doll with woolen guts
spilling out and knotted up
inside the jaws
of parasitic moth larvae.

Somehow
I never thought it strange
that women like me
do not have a hinge for a waist
that we are not built
to bend over and kiss the cushion of our bellies
unless
they have been given over to someone else.

Brigid and her garden

There was a time / when I traveled as a badly-kept secret / passed from mouth to ear / ear to mouth / in whisper-steeped words / in teas of common rue and sunny calendula / mugwort and pennyroyal / Many thought me goddess / Brigid of fertility / bringer of spring / but women knew me as a lover of bodies / a being of opposites / My other name / is gardener / for I know that not everything can grow / I am called / to take merciful shears to the wildest of unwanted twigs / because only then will the moonlight filter in /

Now / however / comes the summer of many centuries / This place has never been Eden / but still / I dislike the graying of things / the dark density of cement / skyscrapers and courthouses / pressing their thickening fingers against the sky / as if they are trapped inside / the only organ we do not own / See, all is overgrown / fumes of pollen / bright-faced petals bruised / autonomy eaten away / by stray roots and insects and codling moths / I am told / that women's lips cannot make the shape of my name / anymore / First the B / too impossibly swollen / for a new, green bud / does not properly unfurl / so that even as the mouth widens from R to I / nothing has presented its sticky flesh / to be cut by the guillotine / of the letter D /

On the bench / outside an abandoned clinic / I met some such unspoken women / *We are for the taking*, they explained / and when I asked what that meant / one woman pulled open her coat to show me that she did not have a belly / only a hook / affixed below her rib cage / on which hung a bloody purse / flushed and oozing as an overripe fruit /

1:00 a.m.

8:00 p.m.
Gives us puddles of light to wade in.
Knee-deep or cocooned in streetlights,
we cast tulle outlines, shadow-sandbags
that drag behind our ankles,
and spill dark tally marks into gutters that froth at the mouth.
It's late enough that one flicker
in the corner of your eye
feels like those times when you plunge into murky water
and something brushes past your foot.

9:00 p.m.
Our parents talk of headlines.
Their faces grow bitter as they sit
like bags of tea, oversteeped,
deepening to floods of bruised blue, earl grey,
while they warn
of daughters who ran, who hitchhiked, who stepped outside
and were eaten by the dark or by the ground.
Don't walk alone, they say,
and stare into their brimming mugs.

10:00 p.m.
And we cannot laugh it off anymore
because the clicks of shutting doors and exiting steps feel like
foreshadowing, feel like those times when you wake up falling
and land, like a stone, in a bed of ripples.

We are tired of the brewing night.
Of our inability to promise that, tomorrow, our names will not be
newsprint,
that, in the morning,
we will drink the dregs of ink and be relieved.

11:00 p.m.
If footprints were syllables, our soles might have inked
panicked pages of poems into the pavement by now,
and every corner
that was more of
an opportunity to run,
every clenched key that carved a scar into the pigment of the dark,
every faked call or location shared on a glowing, palm-sized screen,
every girl who went out anyways, obstinate as a grave,
might have written us in, penned our fear into a sidewalk manuscript.

12:00 a.m.
Is when the hands of clocks begin to fall like coffin lids.
Call us dramatic,
but we have already glimpsed ourselves dead and dug up,
bodies brackish with baseless blame,
scattered, cold, clawed,
we've had to imagine it all.
And whose fault is that,
that any one of us could become the stroke of a pen or a mouthful of mud
that we have already written our epitaphs.

1:00 a.m.
Is for those of us who understand
what lurks between the lines
of texts that say

did you get home safe?

instead of butterflies

suddenly, i am aware of my
breath, of the way my smile lines
warm and deepen, of my two
crumpling hands, and of my
bright eyes, gossamer,
lace border moths drawn
to flame when
i see
her.

the gravity in their pockets

frightened young women punctuate with apologies, carry pebbles in the hems of their skirts and let them grow heavy, walk fast past glowing windows and decide that they are too unwanted to bother making 1, 2, 3 taps of music against the glass, avoid all catalysts, would rather build cairns than skip stones, buy clothing in opaque, say *please* and *thank you* and *sorry* and blame themselves for everything, take long walks along the willamette and collect more pebbles, cradle them like handfuls of plucked petals, say *they love me, they love me not,* practice avoidance, never throw their pebbles, would hate to be as disappointing as a chipped button or a stone that turns dull when it dries or an agate reclaimed by the tide from beneath a beachcomber's fingertips, remain afraid of being made permanent by sculpture, of being broken open like a geode, collect more pebbles, insist that they do not deserve to throw them, sleep in fetal position because it feels like the closest they will ever get to fitting inside the cavity of someone's chest.

How to Cry (Rivers and Other Bodies of Water)

1. You are a brimming jar. Offer droplets of your insides, infrequent as the tides (you cannot be honest all at once).
2. Find fiction: a classic tragedy or cinematic masterpiece to justify your flooding.
3. Hover above the steam of scorched leaves so your eyes can conjure the Dead Sea into a teacup.
4. Let yourself be rocked, a runaway in the iron arms of a railcar, let everyone assume you have been made nauseous by homesickness and not by water, turned sailboat from the inside out.
5. The advantage of living in a time where all flags fly at half-mast? Sob beneath one, and no one will ask,
6. What happened? (You cannot respond to this question.)
7. Stay in your childhood bed, nestled like the fisher's estuarine moths sleeping in your head, in the crevices between ribs that remain as dark as Hadal's layer of the ocean.
8. Bury your face in your hands so you might wring out rhyme and prose and sanguine syllables, so a bit of yourself can escape through the ravine that runs between forefinger to thumb to bless an estuary.
9. Pour it all into a poem, call it your Medusa, show it to no one else for fear that they will turn to sinking stone.
10. Put on a smile or a frozen expression, hide yourself and hope that someone will notice you are leaking rust, and open your lid, and raise you up. (Left alone, you are an anchor drowning in your own throat.)

i am always counting heart beats

first: thursday, i walked 11.5 miles in my bedroom.

second: when my legs began to ache, i laid on the carpet for 120 seconds
and stared at the slanted ceiling

      tap   *tap*   buttons into a bottomless jar   plastic against glass
          get up.

third: i need more steps.   500   400   300   200   100
on one hand   split   to 25 between my fingers   5   4   3   2   1
done   for now.

fourth: algebra was easier than this   when things were not yet limitless

fifth: it really is painstaking   pains taking
counting out sit-ups   and days   and calories   and calculating
pinned   between the numbers that make so much sense on a page

sixth: ribs creak   pink tendons rub raw   slap thin meat   pulled taut
while those parts that cannot   be molded   into brutal handfuls of elastic
must bend too far   must splinter   into bleach white   impaling itself

      heart   *beat*

seventh: jutting hips   pillowy cheeks   proximity to bones   flushed
warm   cold feet   beads of sweat   red on a spidery blue string
plateau of a bruised knee   claret seeping underneath

heart   *beat*

eighth: coils of intestines   infested   the spinal cord   a contorted
centipede   and when i breathe in   my lungs   my insides
flushed and fluttering like panicked blood-vein moths
seethe with the tearing awareness that my body has yet to break

heart   *beat*

ninth: i use buttons to count the days that I succeed
in pushing myself through stinging tedium

freedom is arrhythmic

numbers are comforting   addictive

i cannot trust myself to live by any other metric.

A Dead Fish Meets Her Archaeologist

I knew some archaeologist would dig up my body years from now.
Underground, did you ever find masks or faces
(or did you meet people)?
Ha, ha, ha, handfuls of salt, flesh like an apricot, drained and dried.
Imagine fish, pulled whole from the split hull of a barrel. Cleaver to head,
to hands, to eyes, who goes here?
(Only you.)
Be surprised, drop your tools and gape,
stare so long your eyes roll like marbles from their sockets.

You breathe while I cannot
(but only for so long).
There is peace down here, but you pull part of me from the ground
with the string of a fishing rod. Breakage of a hermetic seal,
I knew an archeologist would find me somewhere.
First, we'll walk riverfronts and cliff edges
and dig hands into each other's flesh like knives into apples.
There is pectin under my fingernails. What do bruises spell out?
Break my neck and find out, find a valley there. We are too high up to fall
(we will fall slowly).

To live, fallen acrobats flop and twist like hot metal. See if
spines burn glyphs and centipedes into a palmar cushion.
Shall I speak of screams?
Shall I speak to you, the archeologist I knew would find me?
Toss laundry into larynx. Hang me up

by a severed thread, then drop me like a writhing puppet.
Forehead to the ground
(we place our foreheads on the ground),
walk away with burning pale faces, and? Be alone, forget you dug me up,
walk around with a clamshell mouth and see what poison falls in.
We will see each other again;

Circus Accident

The ringmaster in my head seems to have wandered off. Enter now, and you will meet chaos, the expansion of a billowing space, yawning pleats falling into place to accommodate frenzied choreography. Find me, the onlooker, lost between circus stripes and whisper-cracks of neuron and synapse. Find me, the unwilling flier, caught up in a trapeze act, crashed down and cut by the shards of a funhouse mirror, then carried off by a swarm of glowing girls through the palace of a dying queen. Find me, the amnesiac, wide-eyed, then suddenly terrified, as the swollen silk walls close in and I become a pickled curiosity, compressed like a contortionist, a whole fruit or a dead animal that finds itself crammed into a jar.

Mithridatism

We have some toxin in our bloodstream, some ritual that wicked its way in
and made us carriers of a grandmother's bitterness,
gave us a taste for dangerous medication.
That is to say, our remedies have always been strange,
our dosages extreme,
we treat chemical deficiencies
of serotonin and dopamine
with self-sabotage,
the killing agent
that collects beneath a glass exterior.
You see,
once we were witches
who trained our fingertips so they would not flinch beneath flames,
so we might tame the pain of burning
before building pyres to step into.
Once we were sleepy weavers
who took up shovels,
spun silken swaths of coffin
swung from apple trees
and buried ourselves whole.
Once we were herbalists,
once we were mothers,
once we were queens, taking arsenic wafers
and painting our faces with lead-white makeup.
Again and again,
a legacy of reckless mithridatism,
of dancing hand-in-hand with death

knowing we could only go so long
without him stepping on our toes.
I suppose I come from generations of women
who sought escapism,
who could never distinguish painkillers from poison,
so that now I am one of too few girls
who proved themselves wrong
when they thought they would not make it to eighteen;

roadkill

i have grown used to existing in my own aftermath,
to walking that neon tightrope
line that divides lanes of traffic
to find that the only way to make it out of the dark
is as a hitchhiker with a reckless thumb,
following the spill of light pollution to the edges of I-5
and risking collision.
it would take less than a second
for me to become somebody's collateral damage,
left to stagger off,
a meal for the flies,
carcass pointed out by passengers behind car windows
until the day they decide
they would rather not watch me rot, would rather not see what they had done.
they would roll me over a steep grade into the ravine-cemetery
where all the unburied girls are kept,
girls who fell like comets, left pockmarks in cement,
who threw themselves into the paths of tire tracks,
so that now, when asked,
people say *she wanted it to end with a car wreck,*
well i say, fuck that.
how dare they build their roadways,
how dare they flash their brights and drive fast past lonely figures
who call out from the shadowy shoulders of interstates,
leave us stranded
then call us selfish

when we step forward
and freeze like deer in headlights,
like moths flown too close to a flame.
they do not even want to visit us.
nobody does
except for little sisters who carry their matted handfuls of dandelions,
who follow muddy footsteps too close to bloody highways.
well i say, do not worry,
little sister,
i will not let you take after me,
and because to say i'd die for you
isn't saying very much,
you know i'll stay for you
because i cannot bear the thought
that you might find me, rotting,
that you might join us, roadside.

my name is a plural noun

between the two of us

                                       i am trying to live.

the twin cut by consonants embedded

                                       in insecticide and

in this cranial asylum
deserves

                                       to rescind

every name

                                       our many names

eve, witch, pig, bitch, dead-girl-walking.

                                    i deserve to leave behind

every reminder like

                                    fingerprints against glass

oven doors that turn alchemists
to lead instead of gold

                                          called

inevitable
car exhaust
or plummeting like death's head hawkmoths
stones in overcoat pockets
river-swallowed

                                      promises
bodies

                                  instead of keepsakes.
                                      in the end,
                       i may be strong enough to say

we all know how poets die.
we all know.

                                        no. no.

Paper Cut, Papercut

I became a seamstress at age three because / although the needle bit my fingers more often than it did the fabric / I wanted so badly to be like my mother / to bury my wrist in her glass jar and pick out buttons / or take brass scissors to vintage sewing patterns / crafting paper dolls that would rarely last / torn apart by my eagerness / into scraps of spare skin.

Dressing rooms soon taught me that people are made of the thinnest paper / stiffening with every button estranged at their back / as if they've been pin-pricked / paper cut / slits in a tailor's mannequin / every daughter / stepping on cracks / wanting to implode into the empty space delineated by side seams and pattern pieces.

I began to spend my summers trying on different measurements / but even reinvention never looked right / left me marking out dotted lines and fisheye darts / inked reminders across my arms / here is where you fold and here is where you cut and here is where you stitch yourself back up.

Still in high school / I did costume fittings / met my pen / my reflection / and my ignorant muse / sewed on extra buttons for a girl who tugged handfuls of elastic from her waistline / insisting / *I wish I could fit into that other dress* / Looking back / I should have admitted everything then / explained that we are easy to cut but harder to mend / that she should not treat herself like a person with seam allowances.

Uninvited

It always catches me off guard, the way I'll be making small talk, hear a self-deprecating comment, and suddenly I'm fourteen again and setting a place for Hunger at the dinner table.

She arrived with the conviction of someone who'd always been there, making it easy for me to overlook her lack of etiquette, the resting of her elbows, her ability to overstay an invitation. And so what if I kept filling up her outstretched palms, spread wide as morning glories, as white porcelain saucers, day by day, exchanging one kind of emptiness for another? So what if her appetite intensified, her famine driving me to carve more meals from the starved corners of cupboards?

With time, I try not to greet her anymore, try to ignore the scars that her knuckles bury in my door and the din of silverware that she'd like to dig into me, spoons into stomach, knives into thighs. Instead, I weave pink perennial sprays into my braids and plan beach days, drink diet pepsi and call my moms and laugh louder than the rattling of plates. I do anything to distract myself from the fact that she'll be back, that she'll linger like mold, doily-blossoms across yellow wallpaper, chipped paint and pockets made by rain, like the smell of rotting fruit or the petals that waste away and grow brown on the bathroom floor, that bleed their funeral-scent and pigment-stains into aged linoleum.

I hate that I am the one who let her in and now all I can say is
getoutofmyhead getoutofmyhead getoutofmyhead.

The things that stay buried

Years from now, some archaeologist will dig me up, pin my remains above a museum plaque, and make me an enigma of crushed stone and broken bone, spiderwebs and exoskeletons, spotlight specimen suspended between white pillars. Years from now, I will become my tangible half, a cryptic artifact whose greatest accomplishments were dying and being found intact. And yet, do not forget, there are things that die but do not stay buried, *and* there are things that stay buried but will never be dead. So years from now, *what then?* There will be things that only I know, but let that be enough; let me be unreadable.

THEY LIKE TO KILL US OFF

They do not write our happy endings. Tragedy is easier to sell.
TRAGEDY   flies off the shelves   faster than beach reads
and ermine moths and the westward sprint of the California gold rush,
so why   would they mind the casualties, the bodies left like
fresh ties on train tracks. After all,   a woman getting killed off
can easily be branded as punishment or bad luck,   and ISn't
her blood biblical, and isn't her funeral ROMANTIC,   and
doesn't melancholia have cinematic potential   or whatever. I
MEAN TO SAY, as long as the dirt is birthing orchards and burying
ribs,   WHO CARES IF there are no midwives to spare, to pick
up fallen apples, I mean to say   I've heard that history hates
lovers, but really, history hates WOMEN and women who love each other,
it is   uninteresting   to DIE HAPPY.   I mean
to say, there must be a witch hunt or a gruesome accident or some
starlet who is impaled by a spit and can fit an apple in her crimson
mouth or else   IT ISN'T ENTERTAINING,   which is the
point, right?   Anyways, now they all boast about their green
thumbs, now that they have gone industrial and begun   to build
trees out of steel and scrap metal,   after all,   they need us
on a larger scale,   they know there is something SO succulent
and feminine about corpses, don't you think, which is why Marilyn went
missing, which is why apple pie has always felt all-American, I mean to
say, THEY LIKE TO KILL US OFF, they like to believe that WE ARE the
kind to arrive in bushels and bear the sinking of their teeth, they like
to give and then take back, to fulfill their favorite tropes, to skip to the
last pages of books to separate the sapphics and go window shopping

for the next DISPOSABLE heroine. I mean to say, the victimology is transparent, I mean to say, it hasn't gotten better, I mean to say, if there really was such a thing as redemption, Eve would already have taken the transcontinental railroad back to Eden and found herself a GODDAMN girlfriend.

Antithetical Bookworms

To me, you spoke before opening your mouth
like a book at the front of a library shelf,
not him, not her, not them, but you
ignorant muse with the illegible title
made wind chimes of my ribs
had me wrapped like twine around your ring finger.

And there I was,
paper eater boring holes and collecting dust,
nothing but a backbone, two covers,
and letters like tiny skeletons
ready to collapse into someone's palms
and be articulated back into cartilage and cursive.

And what if
we took up pens and needles and printed new script,
fixed every gnawed-away page and disguised the patchwork
with scrawls of ink from our fingertips,
typeface that oscillates and falls into place
like writhing invertebrates.

And what if
all there is to know
must be written over and over again
by people like you and I
who find each other and do not mind the time
spent mending book spines and binding new ones.

The thread is not what makes us whole again

They do not tell us that our grandparents killed themselves.
They do not like to talk   about the car crash   the disease   the receipts.
It is understandable that we do not air everything,
that we bury each other like stitches
beneath the grassy duvet of the family plot   beneath tongues
or even tucked into the buttonhole of withering lips,
once young   ruched   and rhododendron pink,
now strained taut   and gray from tasting dust.
Yet, whoever taught us to sew
failed to mention that seams gape
when you take hold of a loose end and pull,
that a frayed edge
will spit out those things we tried to forget
and stitch them into conversation.
Then, we end up biting down on cheekfuls of needles that dig
outwards in channels through the skin, appearing
embedded in wrinkled grimaces.
We are bloodletting   makeshift   worn   ironic;
what family isn't?
With age, we've learned to thread   to knot   to cut   to talk,
calling to be stitched back up in the ringing language of scissors
and silver pins spilled on a countertop.
After all, mending requires us
to pierce pieces of ourselves,
to tear apart in places and turn into moth-eaten grandmothers
so that we do not become undone;

bleeding out

stay awake on those rare days when the sky wears its apron with all
the bloody handshakes, when it lines the horizon with streaks of red
fingerpaint and glares from behind a blush of orange smoke and heat
haze. the atmosphere is quick to bruise, many hues of acrylic changing
to the ruddy indigo of dusk, then deepening to shades of noir and rust,
so do not drift off. you must look up fast, let your shadow be cast upon
the ground like a splash of claret, the mirage of a crime scene that has
yet to be taken into butcher paper or outlined in tape. you may hate the
imprint of your shape, the way you take up space, but do not mistake the
red stain of your silhouette for another jane doe, disappeared into the
dark crevices of bodily topography. do not become woven over by roads
like capillaries, by blistered skin and seeping stomachs and twin kidneys.
do not be lulled by the sanguine sigh of an exposed throat or the soft
snap of cartilage, by the yielding of day into night, the slowing of your
breath, or the closing of your eyes. if nothing else, stay awake and
remember this: you are the heart of everything, a slick cavity that hums
loudly with the effort of feeding, of bleeding your being into everything
that surrounds, but you beat nonetheless.

when girls fly

red satin between my knees. white ribbons across my thighs. one high
heel, lying next to the brake pedal. scratched paint   gasoline   blistered
feet   upholstery that parts ways with the ceiling. on evenings
like these, i want time to stop moving   want it to still and fill
the space between breaths   until i am suspended in momentary
momentum   lungs strained by the excess of a necessity   like
nylon billowing above a blaze of helium.   then, i can drive away
floating   knowing   that i have begun to explode like a
geode into full-blown metamorphosis   fledgling turned acrobat
shedding coats and eyespots   flinging bare legs and throwing
hips   happy, and in love with the simplicity of being happy
acknowledging the stomach-flutter of moths when i see   them
and having a name for it.

now   my only wish   is that i would have flown earlier
would have learned my lesson and taken fists to the killing jar with
the picket fence   instead of letting myself suffocate. i can barely
remember   the crabapple tree with the view of thirteenth street
          bedsheets in the breeze or springwater pavement beneath
my feet.   only the risk   the gifting of my feathers   and the
distance from the ground   altitude that left me heaving.

i think that too many girls have met cliffs   and tried to shrink themselves
to weightlessness. rather than fly, they flee   trip over their own
feet   tumble off a ledge in an ovation of silk and avian corpses
thrashing birds too small for their wings.   i think that too few of us had

someone   to coax our kite strings   to tame our sails and call out
our names   and explain that the wind does not want our
bones to be hollow   to suggest   that we were never afraid of
heights   we were simply afraid of falling;

Sentences.

I am afraid for the day I forget the last of their mannerisms—the way
they walk, the shape of their jaw, the shadows that soft hairs cast
onto their forehead, the constellation of freckles on their cheek, their
sunburnt legs, their chipped nail polish, and the way they bob their head
when they laugh, and weave beads into their shoelaces, and rest their
left ankle on their right knee—if asked, I would talk about them in many
run-on sentences and hope that we remain endless in the time it takes
to reach the closing punctuation of my recollections.

I could have sworn I met my ghost at fifteen

and she looked young like me
brown braids and apples in her cheeks
blue veins that crawled like vines beneath pale skin
bursting to carnations in her fists.
Between bouquet and grave face
she looked like a girl arriving at her own funeral.
I think I mistook my reflection
for foreshadowing
because I greeted her like she was spectral friend
who came to deliver our eulogy.

Somehow, I kept her impatient
realized that I did not have to stay haunted
that I could cut her tether with my shoulder blade
and let her spill
scattered pearls and raw milk between floorboards
that we could fade like film negatives:
one, the afterimage embedded in my eyelid
the other, living and withering like a ripening fruit.

Now, with time,
I'm beginning to forget about that echo of my outline.
Maybe I'll dance with a bride in a twin ivory dress
luna moths beneath streetlamps, exhalations of ash and baby's breath
until I do not need to rob graves to rest my head in stone
until my scalp is stained by moonlight
and my skin draws into itself like the gathering of tulle into ruffles.

a trick of the light

Someone lit a candle in my stomach,
and now I search palms for a sheen of wax,
for evidence of who made me this way,
                    brief and fragile as one thin flame.
It's as if some puppeteer
stands above me, his shears
biting at a frayed ribbon of smoke,
threatening to trim my wick and watch me tire
to a waning curl of kindling,
snapped as a matchstick,
I feel the collapsing of many legs.

So it goes,
        or so you tell me,
but I hate that lately I've been feeling temporary,
just as shadows trail a step behind
and thunder claps its hands at lightning's back,
how the sun beams a momentary green
and bullets crack their muzzle flash,
how a dying star will leave its bright fingerprint behind,
I, too, am a trick of lagging light
        that flutters
        like a firefly
        in a rib cage.

So I ask you, if we were moths, to what light would we be drawn?
Promise me a slow burn
or else let us erupt,
stippled into nothingness like a winged display of sparks.

I refuse to be The Entomologist

The Puppeteer,
The Archeologist,
or any other given name
that may have tasked me
with my own entrapment,
a body, stagnant
swarm of stars beneath the glass
of an open casket
waiting
to be relinquished
by the turning of a page.
Even as hand and paper disintegrate
into wings
beetles and Baily's beaded monarchs
and other crawling things
I do not want to draw them
into my own terrified orbit.
I do not want to burn out
like a screaming asterism
I do not want to tear the hearts from my sleeves
and replace them with insects,
wingtips mounted to my wrists.
I would like to be
a soft, simple miracle
the eclipse of moths
that begin, bound up in nothing but their own shapeless cloth
and later transform into something that is dull gray and ordinary,
but oddly, enough;

Author's Note on Mental Health

I began writing this chapbook without the belief or expectation that it would ever be published. However, now that I have the privilege to see it in print, now that a small part of me has been made tangible, I realize it may reach an audience that has similar mental health experiences to my own. If this feels true for you, know that you are more than deserving of unconditional help.

If you do not feel safe or ready to confide in people in your life, YouthLine (theyouthline.org) is an excellent (Oregon-based but nationally available) teen-to-teen crisis/mental health chat service. Their volunteers will communicate online or call and text via 877-968-8491 from 4-10pm PST. After hours, phone calls transfer to 988, the national suicide and crisis hotline. I can also personally speak to the merits of The Trevor Project (thetrevorproject.org), which offers similar services that cater specifically to LGBTQ+ youth. They have counselors at the ready 24/7 for phone calls (1-866-488-7386) and texts (678-678). Both organizations are anonymous and confidential to a point—see websites for more details.

To every reader, artist, poet, young person . . . I am sending my love. I hope that you find your silver lining, as I did in writing this book. I hope that you, too, are learning to refuse the role of The Entomologist.

CLARA MCAULEY (she/her) is a
queer poet from Portland, Oregon.
Having graduated high school in
2023, she is now studying Pre-Med
Biology and Creative Writing at
Lehigh University, where she
intends to costume theater
productions, rant about social
justice issues, and perform aerial
silks in her spare time. Her work
has previously been published in
The Song Between Our Stars and *Up
North Literary Journal*, and it can
also be found on her instagram,
@moths_and_poetry.

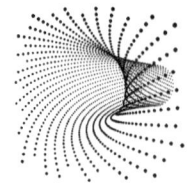

FIRSTMATTERPRESS
Portland, Ore.

*Founded in 2018 to dissolve publication barriers for
first-time publishing poets and genre-expanding writers.*

2024
FEATURED COVER ARTIST ALEXANDRA STRENFEL

GREENHOUSE
sophie hall

SUSPENDED IN MY INSECTICIDE JAR
clara mcauley

2023
FEATURED COVER ARTIST LARA ROUSE

FLOATING BONES
rae diamond

TEN-CENT FLOWER & OTHER TERRITORIES
charity e. yoro

OUR FAVORITE PEOPLE IN THE ROOM
edited by ash good, lauren paredes & emily moon

2022
FEATURED COVER ARTIST RACHEL MULDER

BETWEEN THESE BORDERS WANDERS A GOLEM
ahuva s. zaslavsky

EVEN THE AIR, TOO HEAVY
riley danvers

ONE ROW AFTER / BIR SIRA SONRA
sonya wohletz

SOMEONE I CAN HOLD GENTLY
xylophone mykland

STORIES FOR WHEN THE WOLVES ARRIVE
hailey spencer

2021
FEATURED COVER ARTIST ALEKSANDRA APOCALISSE

CONSIDER THE BODY, WINGED
jessica e. pierce

ROUTES BETWEEN RAINDROPS
dan wiencek

THE GROWTH LINES
gabby hancher

2020
FEATURED COVER ARTIST SARA SWOBODA

BODY UNTIL LIGHT
k.m. lighthouse

IT'S JUST YOU & ME, MISS MOON
emily moon

LOVERS AND OTHER STILL CREATURES
eitan codish

2019
FEATURED COVER ARTIST HELLSEA

OTHERWISE, MAGIC
lauren paredes

THE NIGHT SKY IS A PLACE WHERE THINGS GET LOST
andrew chenevert

TIME COUNTS BACKWARD FROM INFINITY
k.m. lighthouse

WE ARE NOT READY FOR WHAT WE ARE
ash good

2018
FEATURED COVER ARTIST HOLGER LIPPMANN

SOUNDS IN MY MÖBIUS MIND
ash good

YOU ARE AN AMBIGUOUS PRONOUN
k.m. lighthouse

We are a non-profit writer collective press & our authors maintain 100% of book sale proceeds. Please support independent booksellers by purchasing our titles at Bookshop.org

FIRSTMATTERPRESS.ORG